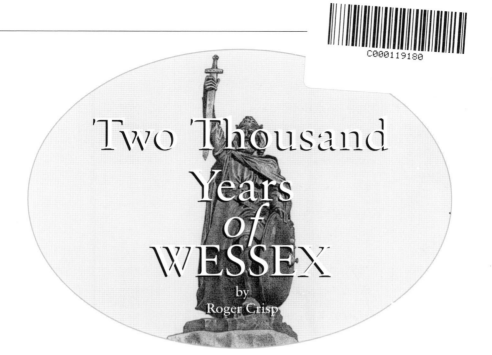

Two Thousand Years of WESSEX

by
Roger Crisp

If you asked people in the south west of England What is Wessex? you might find them 'all in a charm 'n' a puzzivent' about giving you an answer; they would all start talking and bustling together and with different ideas. Anyone who used those exact words would undoubtedly come from Wessex. (Dialect and idiom might be one way of defining Wessex, but since the spread of radio and then television the old ways of talking are harder to come by.)

Logically, Wessex means the land of the West Saxons. As they grew in power so did Wessex until it was bigger than a single county, such as Sussex (South Saxons) and Essex (East Saxons).

In this short book we follow the development of Wessex from the time before the Saxons, through their own era and on up to the present day. The map we are using includes the modern counties of Devon, Somerset, Avon, Wiltshire, West Hampshire, Southern Berkshire, the fringes of Oxfordshire and Gloucestershire, and Cornwall. Cornwall is not generally thought of as part of Wessex – especially by the Cornish. But in fact archaeological evidence suggests that the kingdom of Dumnonia (Devon) was incorporated by the West Saxons around 700BC, and that Cornwall was incorporated into Wessex by King Egbert in the first half of the ninth century.

The Roman Invasion

THE ROMANS · THE SAXONS · SAXON CAPITALS

AD43 the Romans arrive

Below right:

Roman mosaic pavement. High Street, Fordington.

AD410 the Romans leave Britain

Below:

A great earth wall which once stretched from Portishead to Salisbury Plain, was used by the Romano-British against the West Saxons.

AD495 Saxon invasions begin

The Roman invasion of AD43 brought with it huge changes in building skills, road building, arts and public life. The most famous Roman legacy in Wessex is the city of Bath. But other indications of Roman life are also to be found at Rockbourne, Hampshire, and just outside Dorchester. Straight Roman roads are in use even today – the A4 from London to Bristol is a Wessex example.

In many ways Wiltshire, with its wealth of prehistoric sites, can still be regarded as the geographical heart of Wessex. The small market town of Wilton, just west of Salisbury, was the first recognised capital of the West Saxons, and therefore of Wessex. Throughout Wessex only a few buildings remain showing their Anglo-Saxon origins. The small churches at Bradford-on-Avon and Breamore are good examples.

The Saxons arrived, from their German homelands, somewhere along the south coast of Britain and Cerdic led them to victory over the British-Romans they encountered. The area of Charford, near Downton, Wiltshire, and within the parish of the Saxon church at Breamore is reputed to be the site of one of Cerdic's major battles ('Cerdic's ford'), at which 5000 Britons were killed, including their king, who is reckoned to have

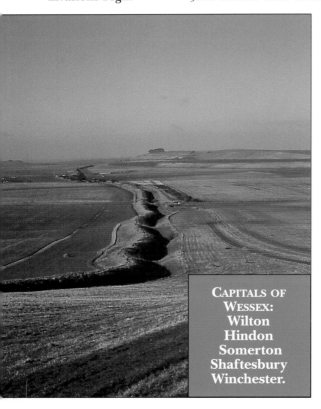

CAPITALS OF
WESSEX:
**Wilton
Hindon
Somerton
Shaftesbury
Winchester.**

been buried in the Long Barrow near Grim's Ditch. (The name Saxon is thought to be derived from their short sword, called a seaxe.)

But this was not a single invasion. Gradually more Saxons came and they spread out in clans and families, not as a great marauding army.

The word king is derived from the Saxon Cyning (kin) and meant the clan or family leader who was elected by the council called the Witenagemote, or the Meeting of the Elders. Folk Moots were local councils. There is still a Moot Garden at Downton on the Wiltshire–Hampshire border.

Left:
The Mortuary Chest of King Egbert, said to be the first king of England, is kept in Winchester Cathedral.

Saxon royal burial sites in Wessex:
Glastonbury
Malmesbury
Sherborne
Wimborne
Winchester
Wareham
Shaftesbury

Egbert is often referred to as the first king of England. During his reign a certain amount of unity became apparent. He was the leader of the West Saxons and therefore of Wessex. By AD827, after the death of Offa, he became Overlord of Mercia and Northumbria as well as King of Wessex. Because Wessex at that time included Kent and Essex he was thus actually King of all England, from the Firth of Forth to Dover.

The Danes, however, were becoming increasingly dangerous from the East, up the Thames, and the south west, at Teignmouth in Devon. Their tentative and successful raids led to the full scale invasions by the fierce and bloodthirsty Norsemen. Much of Egbert's England fell. Wessex was increasingly threatened.

AD802-839 **Egbert of Wessex 'first king of England'**

Alfred the Great

ALFRED THE GREAT AND SUPREMACY OF WESSEX

848 birth of Alfred in Wantage, Berks
871 Alfred becomes King
878 Alfred defeats Danes

Below:

The chalk horse we see today at Westbury was cut in 1778 and looks like a straightforward picture of the animal. However, aerial views seem to show the outline of one of a much more abstract shape, very much like the Bronze Age

During these times of resistance Alfred the Great emerged as the most important leader of Wessex. His campaign against the Danes is the beginning of Wessex as the cradle of England. In AD877 his palace at Chippenham, North Wiltshire, was taken. He retreated all the way over to Somerset. There, at Athelney Island, he regrouped his forces – and probably burnt the cakes too! Making progress eastwards again he routed the Danes. There was a final pitched battle in AD878, popularly believed to have been at Eddington, near Westbury, in West Wiltshire. The story also goes that a white horse was carved in the chalk hillside to commemorate Alfred's own horse.

At the eventual mutual dividing of lands and agreements with Guthrum, the King of the Danes, Alfred had unified Southern England. He was a great leader with or without wars. As a scholar he codified laws, founded around two dozen towns and had many others fortified, he set up schools for the upper classes, designed houses, brought in foreign scholars, and set about restoring and setting up convents and abbeys.

horse at Uffington, in Berkshire. Legend tells us that the older Westbury carving was in commemoration of Alfred's horse.

With his academic skills he managed to learn Latin and translated books into Anglo-Saxon. These, of course, would essentially have been ecclesiastical works. He is even credited with having invented a candle clock. Here was a one-man renaissance, centuries before Italy's, whose triumphant-looking statue stands, sword aloft, in Winchester near the cathedral.

What of the land itself? Many of today's parish boundaries are very close to original Anglo-Saxon land units. These units seem increasingly to have been based upon land divisions set up by and before the Romans. Some land units are thought to date back to prehistoric times.

By the end of the 8th century Wessex had already been divided into administrative shire units which were named after the regional capitals. Dorset derives from Dorchester; Wiltshire from Wilton; Hampshire from Hamwic (Southampton); Somerset from Somerton. Berkshire seems to have been named after the Berroc wood (a box wood) which was found all over the area.

Clues to the origins of settlements can be found in place names. In the same way that -*chester* derives from the Roman word *castra*, castle or camp and *ceastre*, town, so there are many Saxon name endings. Wil-*ton* means farm or homestead of those living on the river Wylye. Alvediston, between Shaftesbury and Salisbury, was the -*ton* of Alfred, or Alfred's Ton. The Saxon name endings of -*ley*, -*leigh*, -*hurst*, -*hay*, -*stoke*, -*fold*, -*bury*, -*worth* all meant a clearing or an enclosure; -*wick*, -*ham* meant settlements; and a -*burh* was a fortified settlement. Having so many burhs (around thirty in Alfred's time) gives a sense of the political unification of Wessex.

Further evidence of Saxon Wessex and England have been found in the document called the Saxon Chronicle, dating from the early 10th century. This was the Saxons' equivalent of the later Domesday Book compiled by the Normans.

A major change took place for Wessex just before the Normans invaded led by William the Conqueror. Until then Winchester was the undisputed capital, politically and ecclesiastically, of Wessex (i.e. Southern England). Then the ruling family split. Queen Emma and Edward the Confessor, her son, fell out. When he came to the throne in 1042 he shifted the emphasis of power towards London, where he founded Westminster Abbey. There he was buried , leaving his brother-in-law, Harold, to face the invading Normans.

Centre:
King Alfred's statue stands in Winchester, the Wessex capital most often associated with him.

Below:
The Roman amphitheatre built on the site of a Bronze Age stone circle known as Maumbury Rings, was used until the Middle Ages for beast-baiting and until the eighteenth century for public executions.

1042 Edward shifts power from Winchester to London

Aug: 22. 1723
Prospect of Dorchester from the Amphitheater.

The Norman Invasion

THE NORMANS; WAR, CATHEDRALS, CASTLES

1066 the Normans invade

Below:

The Norman castle at Corfe, Dorset, was ruined in the Civil War.

The Normans (Norsemen) first of all left their mark by building over most Saxon structures. This is particularly true of the ecclesiastical edifices. Winchester was a major target, of course, and the Norman cathedral stands as testimony today. Bath, Sherborne and Glastonbury were also reshaped. The Normans built comprehensively. Massive stone castles were erected, at Dunster, Bridgwater and Taunton in Somerset; Wardour, Dorchester and Corfe in Dorset; Malmesbury, Old Sarum (Salisbury) and Trowbridge in Wiltshire; and at Windsor, Exeter, Oxford and Carisbrooke on the Isle of Wight, to name but a few. Each dominated huge tracts of the Wessex countryside.

Royal forests and palaces or large manor houses continued the hunting traditions of all previous rulers of Wessex. Clarendon, to the west of Salisbury, was a favourite for centuries, but now only a dilapidated wall remains of the original palace. The New Forest of Hampshire, Savernake Forest of North Wiltshire, Neroche Forest on the Somerset–Devon borders make part of the huge tracts of privileged royal

Left:
The Rufus Stone in the New Forest commemorates the spot where William II, Rufus, was killed by an arrow in the eye in 1100.

...And thereafter on the morning after Lammas day was the king William shot in hunting, by an arrow from his own men, and afterwards brought to Winchester, and buried in the Cathedral

Saxon Chronicle

Below:
Winchester Cathedral, an ecclesiastical Norman powerhouse, stands as historical testimony today.

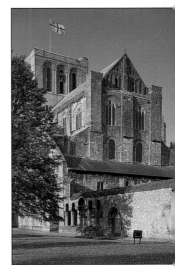

hunting. Interestingly, the term 'forest' did not mean trees in particular. It is derived from the Latin foras, meaning 'out of' or 'outside', because the royal forests were enlarged by taking areas out of the common land and put entirely under the control of the king.

Being the ground of royalty meant that they were also forests of political intrigue. The Rufus Stone in the New Forest commemorates the spot where William II, Rufus, third son of William the Conqueror, was killed by an arrow in the eye in 1100. It brought his reign of thirteen years to an abrupt end. But it has never been clear whether this was a hunting accident or murder.

Landowners and Feudalism

POWERFUL LANDOWNERS – BISHOPRICS,

Right:

The Great Barn at Tisbury is the largest tithe barn in England. It is 200 feet long and supports a great thatched roof.

S trict laws were enforced to keep commoners out of the forests. Henry I, for example, decreed that dogs should all be 'lawed'. Only mastiffs could be kept on royal land and all dogs kept for droving should have two toes cut off to prevent them from hunting the deer.

In other ways, though, he was a practical man. Roger, Bishop of Salisbury, became a great favourite of the king initially, it seems, because of the speed with which he conducted church services!

Ecclesiastical prosperity and dominion

Many of the vast estates of the manor houses included several villages at a time and belonged to the Church hierarchy. The Bishop of Winchester's domains stretched all over Wessex, a legacy of the capital's long-standing influence; Wells and Salisbury were the two other powerful bishoprics and the great nunnery at Shaftesbury also owned a great deal of land.

So much Wessex land under high society ownership meant that there was not much room or allowance made for 'freemen'. Most of the population was under some kind of servitude and very much attached to the land, through which they owed allegiance to the crown. This centralisation became the heart of feudalism. Most farming was under the two-field system. More fertile river valleys and rich claylands, such as in West Dorset, used a three-field system whereby one field was kept fallow each year. In Portland, Dorset, we can still see evidence of this.

**Below:
Salisbury
Poultry Cross**

Wessex has always been associated with farming. Thus many of the centres of population had their own markets. In towns certain crosses often became associated with the selling of certain produce. There is the Poultry Cross at Salisbury, for example. But even small villages had their own markets and crosses where everything was on sale. Bradford Abbas,

Genealogy of the Saxon Kings

near Yeovil, used to have a market cross until about 1800. The site is still called 'The Cross' on the street sign, and Cross Cottage also marks the place. Often these market sites were specifically mounted with a cross to provide a visible conscience and keep traders honest.

The severity of Norman rule brought an outbreak of civil war during Stephen's weak reign. Wessex was very much involved since the unrest began in 1136 at Exeter. The final war, once started, lasted ten years. The land and those closest to it were the major victims. The Welsh and Scots saw the strife and joined the fray. France also attacked under Matilda of Anjou. Armies destroyed crops, cattle and houses in their path all across the region.

1136 civil unrest begins in Exeter

The various lands, castles and estates throughout Wessex from Dunster in the west to Windsor in the east, and from Malmesbury in the north to Portland in the south, belonged to various claimants to the throne, supporting nobility and the Church. Wessex was therefore an entire battlefield. For the ordinary Wessex farmer and peasant the period was quite simply one of horror and total anarchy.

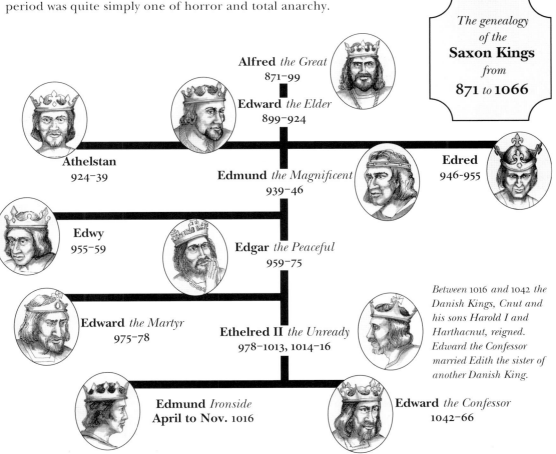

The genealogy of the **Saxon Kings** *from* **871** *to* **1066**

Alfred *the Great*
871–99

Edward *the Elder*
899–924

Athelstan
924–39

Edmund *the Magnificent*
939–46

Edred
946-955

Edwy
955–59

Edgar *the Peaceful*
959–75

Edward *the Martyr*
975-78

Ethelred II *the Unready*
978–1013, 1014–16

Edmund *Ironside*
April to Nov. 1016

Edward *the Confessor*
1042–66

Between 1016 *and* 1042 *the Danish Kings, Cnut and his sons Harold I and Harthacnut, reigned. Edward the Confessor married Edith the sister of another Danish King.*

Winchester's Royal Decline

WINCHESTER GIVES WAY TO WESTMINSTER

Winchester's Royal Decline 1100–1200

Below:
The great moat around the palace of the powerful Bishop of Wells.

During the 12th century another important political development was that Winchester decreased in importance as the centre of royal business. Coronations and crown wearing ceremonies fell by the wayside, particularly after the royal palace was plundered and sacked. A royal treasury remained and royal visits were made for about another century. The last great royal ceremony was the ritual bathing and recrowning of Richard I (the Lionheart) in 1194, after his disastrous Crusades.

New towns developed

With increasing pressure on the land, throughout Saxon and Norman times, to produce more food for consumption as well as for tithes and taxes, more land was being cleared of woods, drained of swamps and even terraced to achieve higher production. The chalkland terraces, or 'strip lynchets', can still be seen throughout much of Dorset, Wiltshire and the White Horse Vale of Berkshire.

Increased production and also prosperity led to a growth in size and range of crafts in the Wessex towns. New towns were built and communications between them were improved.

Wool brought great prosperity to merchants and farmers as Great Chalfield Manor, near Bradford-on-Avon, testifies.

Sheep were an important livestock, for their dung as much as for their wool. Goats were also widely kept. Both flocks would thrive on the light arable lands and especially on the chalk lands which form a central core to Wessex stretching from Abbotsbury, on the Dorset Coast, through Salisbury Plain and on up to the Marlborough Downs. Cattle would use the richer pasture lands of the river valleys where Wessex cheese was a noted dairy product. Pigs were important for the local economy and grain was grown throughout Wessex. Water mills, for grinding corn or for fulling wool were to be found on any suitably fast running water.

Markets and fairs were necessary to exchange produce, as well as an excuse to indulge in life's other pleasures of drinking, dancing and general merriment.

A classic example of this expansion was the founding of New Sarum (Salisbury) in Wiltshire. The city with its castle and cathedral stood originally on the ancient earthwork mound to the north of the present Salisbury, which we now call Old Sarum. Enclosed by a fortified wall by the end of the 12th century there was no further room for expansion, so a new site was proposed. The Abbess of Wilton (the nearby former Wessex capital and important market town) was asked her permission by Bishop Poore to build his new cathedral in her Abbey grounds. She refused. The current site was then chosen, Merrifield (Mary's Field), half way between Old Sarum and Wilton. The magnificent cathedral was built in only 40 years (the spire being added in the 14th century) and the market town grew up around it. So, from 1280 on, Wilton was eclipsed by Salisbury as a trade, craft, ecclesiastical and political centre.

By the mid-14th century many new boroughs had been created throughout Wessex and change was in the air. Increased population meant that more and more working men were solely reliant on earning a wage. They had no land of their own. If crops failed they had no means of growing their own food, nor of working for it and, so, no means of buying what might be available.

New Wessex Boroughs:
Alton
Andover
Basingstoke
Blandford Forum
Bridgwater
Hungerford
Lyme Regis
Marlborough
Newbury
Trowbridge
Wells

1280 **Salisbury eclipses Wilton**

Creation of new boroughs

From Black Death to Lollards

1349 the Black Death arrives

Above:

The Saxon church at Breamore (Hampshire) is a good example of church decoration.
Around the upper walls of the porch are the remains of a large mural of Christ on the cross, overlaid on an older rural scene.

The Black Death, coming from Asia, struck in 1349 and more than halved the national population, which was nearly 4 million. It struck Wessex first, probably having landed from a ship at Melcombe Regis, near Weymouth, in Dorset. Everybody – royalty, nobles, the Church, peasants – felt the effects of recession except for one or two areas in the wool trade which found that exports to France and Europe were increasing. The huge ports of Bristol and Southampton still prospered for a time, but overall the living were unable to deal with burying all the dead and the crops and livestock were left untended. The price of labour rose and the value of land went down. Many farmers subsequently turned their land over to pasture because it was cheaper to pay one shepherd than forty or fifty labourers. Across the whole of Wessex parishes and villages were being deserted and either disappeared altogether or remained just as a single farm.

From then on laws keeping the peasants in virtual slavery were more severe, while the Church and nobility leeched them with taxes and subjugation. Indeed the Church at this time reckoned to have held about one third of the total revenues of the whole country. Unrest with both Church and nobility was on the increase and found philosophical support in the growth of the Lollard Movement. Its main voice was John Wycliffe who, along with other theologians, was appalled at the wealth of the Church and nobility and their usurping of power.

Despite these factors the Church continued to spend vast amounts on itself, its buildings and its estates. Contrary to what we see today the parish churches would have been highly decorated and colourful inside. Some remnants remain in the churches of Gussage St. Andrew (Dorset), the famous 'Doom Painting' inside St. Thomas' Church, Salisbury (Wiltshire), Ditcheat (Somerset), Aldermaston (Berkshire) and Hurstbourne Tarrant (Hampshire). The village records at Bradford Abbas, Dorset, tell us how the nave roof had red and white roses, the beams were painted in stripes of red, white and blue; the chancel roof had a blue background dotted with stars, and that there were several painted angels holding scrolls or shields.

The Lollard Movement came to include all kinds of disaffection with the Church. Debtors, anti-Papists, nonconformists and heretics of all types provided a strong undercurrent of feeling. In 1414 forty tradesmen from Bristol marched to St. Giles in the Fields, London, to join a rally. During the years that followed records tell of various people being tried and imprisoned for offences like distributing Lollard pamphlets (Frome), owning Bibles written in English (Devizes). In 1431 a group attacked Salisbury Cathedral and another attacked Abingdon Abbey. The leaders of both were publicly executed. A further insurrection in Portsmouth in 1450 led to the whole town's being excommunicated for half a century. During Cade's Rebellion, in the same year, the Bishop of Salisbury was dragged from the church at Eddington (site of Alfred's last battle with the Danes), West Wiltshire, robbed and murdered. The mob moved on to attack the Priory. Other areas of Wiltshire witnessed similar scenes: Devizes, Wilton, Tilshead to name only three.

There were continual but disjointed insurrections throughout the century. Ecclesiastical courts, which were similar to Inquisitions, tried the cases. (Catholicism was the religion of England at this time.) These conveniently decided that being in any way against the Church equalled heresy. Failure to repent from heresy meant execution and from 1401 this had meant being burned at the stake. This was not a cheap method, as has been documented in records of the time. One thoughtful lady actually left a fund to the city of London for this very purpose! Ironically this was the period we generally talk of as 'Merrie Englande'.

The Lollards did not go away. In 1514, the court at Salisbury tried cases from all over Wiltshire. The ideas the movement stood for ran deep and were not religiously motivated at all. The three main demands were that serfdom should be abolished; that heavy taxes should be cancelled; and that the Church's grip on the land should be weakened.

> 'When Adam delved and Eve span, where was then the gentleman.'

The Lollards

1450 Cade's Rebellion

Left:
Salisbury Cathedral, which has the tallest spire and largest cathedral close in England.

1514 Wiltshire Lollards tried in Salisbury

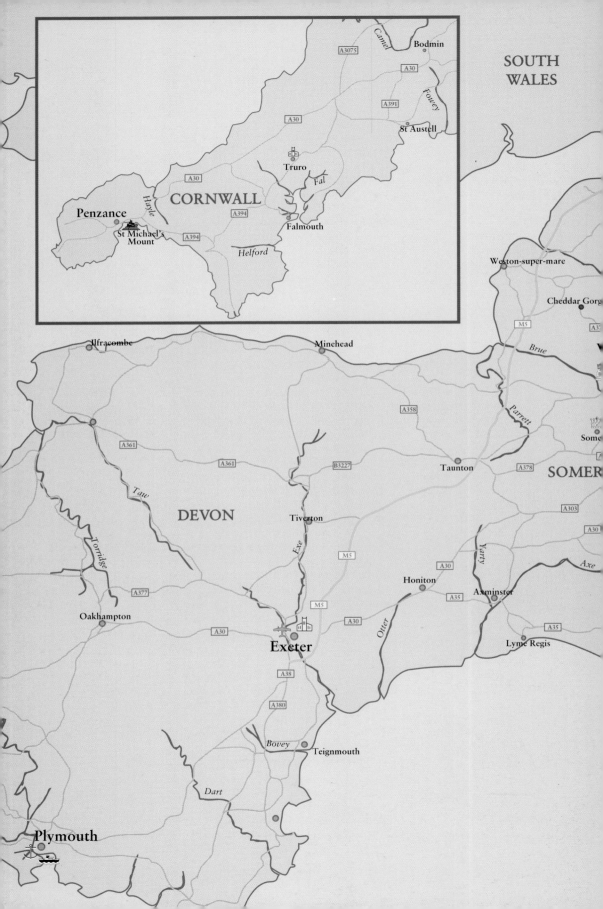

A417
A429
Oxford
A46
OXFORDSHIRE
Cirencester
A419
A338
Abingdon
GLOUCESTERSHIRE
M5
A419 A420
Wantage
Malmesbury
Uffington
(White Horse)
Swindon
A429 M4
BERKSHIRE
M4
M4
A338
M4
Chippenham
A429
A345
Reading
Calne
Windmill Hill
Avon
Avebury
Marlborough
Avon
Silbury
(Stone Circle)
Hill
A342
Savernake
Hungerford
Newbury
Bath
A4
A4
Bradford-on-Avon
Devizes
A346 A338
A4
Trowbridge
A342
A343
A361 A350
A360
Basingstoke
Westbury
WILTSHIRE
A338
Frome
A342
Andover
hepton Mallet
A361
Warminster
Test
ury
Wylye
Stonehenge
(Prehistoric Site)
A34
A359
Hindon
A338
A30
M3
A303
Wilton
A272
A31
orth Cadbury
A350
Salisbury
Winchester
A30
Shaftesbury
Test
A30
Romsey
A350
Itchen
M3
Sherborne
Rockbourne
M27
Hamble
A354
Cranborne
HAMPSHIRE
Southampton
Meon
rne Abbas
Blandford Forum
A31
Ringwood
Beaulieu
M27
Giant
DORSET
A31
A30
Wimborne
A354
Minster
Lymington
A31
Dorchester
Poole
Avon
Maiden
Piddle
Portsmouth
Castle
Frome
Wareham
Isle of Wight
Swanage
Weymouth
Portland Bill

	Capitals of Wessex
	Royal burial sites
	Roman sites
	Railway centre
	Naval ports
	Trading ports

Trade and Farming

TRADE IMPROVES · ROADS, BRIDGES AND PORTS ARE BUILT

1415 resumption of Hundred Years War

Below:

Water Meadows at Salisbury, originally made as a means of irrigation.

From the 13th century inland trade had brought about an improvement in communications. The increase in the number of boroughs and towns in Wessex, where the markets and fairs were held, shows this. Getting to these important fairs and markets meant crossing rivers and this encouraged the building of bridges. Many fine medieval bridges are still as important as they ever were. Harnham Bridge on Salisbury's south side provided a link straight down to Blandford Forum and the south coast, taking trade away from the ancient market town of Wilton. The medieval bridge at Coombe Bissett is on the same road.

Other fine examples of bridges can be found at Castle Combe and Bradford-on-Avon in North Wiltshire, and at Abingdon, on the Thames, which drew the Oxford-bound traffic away from Wallingford.

When the Hundred Years War resumed in 1415, the whole of the South Wessex Coast became important in the fight against the French. Southampton was the major naval centre and the inland roads carried a different traffic. This was really where the Royal Navy began to be a formidable force. Under Henry VIII, in the following century, Portsmouth became established as the major naval port on the south coast.

Inevitably, the story of life in Wessex always returns to the land. Various travellers, writers and farmers have given us their impressions. Large flocks of sheep were still, in the 17th century, essential to the growing of corn. Wheat and barley were the most profitable of the crops but the fertilisation of the soil by the sheep was an integral part of the

Another important agricultural development was the making of 'water meadows', essentially a means of irrigation. Many of the fast chalk streams suited this purpose. The Test and Itchen in Hampshire, the Piddle in Dorset, and the Wylye and Avon in Wiltshire. In Salisbury to this day, walking from the Elizabeth Gardens to the Old Mill at Harnham takes you past fields still known by locals as the Water Meadows, where the sluice gates and the gentle undulations caused by the narrow water channels are plain to see.

process. The shepherd, tramping the open chalk uplands in all weathers, his dog at his side, was thus a man of great responsibilities. Often he was responsible for the life of his sheep on pain of losing their value from his wages.

Comparison of the chalklands with the dairy farming and high cheese production of the fertile river valley areas must have given rise to the well-known phrase, 'as different as chalk from cheese'. John Aubrey, Wiltshire's

Below:
The bridge of Bradford-on-Avon was on the medieval trade route.

delightful 17th-century antiquarian, found that the temperaments of the people differed too. The dairymen he found more melancholy and malicious than the shepherds, who were more measured and straightforward in their speech.

Away from the chalk uplands in the 16th and 17th centuries farming was either fully mixed or predominantly dairy in the river areas. The western uplands of the Quantocks, the Mendips, the reclaimed Somerset levels, and the Dorset and New Forest Heaths specialised more in raising stock, horses and cattle.

By the beginning of the 17th century hops and brewing were found in several places: Salisbury (Wiltshire), Alton and Romsey (Hampshire), and Dorchester (Dorset). This is still the case in most of them.

Trades and the Church

CRAFTS IN THE COTTAGES

Of other trades, cloth making was perhaps the most important throughout Wessex, in such places as Bradford-on-Avon, Trowbridge and Westbury, in Wiltshire; Frome, Keynsham, Dunster, Taunton and Bath, in Somerset; and Sherborne and Lyme Regis in Dorset. Of course there was still farming, but the small dairy farms allowed for a second kind of employment in the cottages. In other words, if there was no corn there was cloth. Much of it was exported, especially to France, Ireland and Spain. The highest quality products, from Bradford-on-Avon and Frome, for example, were sent to London.

By the same token, the cloth exporters were also big importers of foods, oils, wines and dyestuffs for the domestic markets. The domestic wool was not of very high grade. Gradually Spanish wool became a necessary import as tastes for finer cloths and draperies were increased. Silk weaving was even introduced and lacemaking was another strong cottage industry. This was particularly so in South Wiltshire and around Blandford Forum and Lyme Regis in Dorset.

The reign of Henry VIII was largely notable for the break with Rome and for the Dissolution of the Monasteries. Then, in 1553, 'Bloody' Mary took the throne and her first royal act was to reinstate Catholicism. Elizabeth I followed, in 1558, and reversed the legislation, reinstating Protestantism. The ordinary people seem to have got on with their lives believing that, either way, God was intimately part of their everyday life.

Life in the parish churches was even less affected. The churchyards had always been sites of fairs, village parties, games, maypoles, wrestling and other sports. Schools were also held in churches. The village church of North Cadbury, Somerset, has the remains of the alphabet on the wall of the vestry. Education of a more adult kind is evident on the wall of Breamore's Saxon church where a stone simply says: 'Avoyd Fornication'!

Puritanism put paid to the vibrant life of the churches, and royal taxation and ship taxes for defence against the Spanish, Dutch and French were deeply unpopular. Increasingly the tax collectors found that they were unable to find people rich enough to pay.

**1539 Henry VIII and the Reformation
1553 Mary I Catholic
1558 Elizabeth I Protestant**

Below:

The King's House, in Salisbury Cathedral Close, is now the home of the Salisbury and South Wilts Museum, and repository of many local trade products.

Left:
This stumpwork mirror frame of c.1670 was reputedly made in Amesbury, Wiltshire, for Charles II and Catherine of Braganza.

From Civil War to 'Bloody Assizes'

Major Civil War battles in Wessex

1643 1645	Bridgwater
1645	Chippenham
1643 1644	Newbury
1644	Cheriton
1643 1644	Poole
1644	Abbotsbury
1644	Wardour

Right:
Remains of Wardour Castle, one of a number of magnificent buildings sadly destroyed during the Civil War.

Clubmen strong in Wessex by 1645

1685 Monmouth Rebellion halted at Sedgemoor

The Civil War was coming and with it came a huge and disastrous effect upon Wessex. The deep south-west was largely Royalist and the King's headquarters were at Oxford. In between were Parliamentarian strongholds. Furthermore the Wessex Channel Ports were of strategic importance to both sides as depots and as contact points for communication and military supply, and for trading with the Continent.

As is usually the case, the common people wanted to get on with their lives and make ends meet. But the constant to and fro of armies caused widespread destruction and disruption since they were often little more than licensed thieves. Merchants and tradesmen were largely neutral and simply wanted it all over as quickly as possible. Peasants and workers likewise lived in constant fear of losing what little they had.

This helplessness left a kind of vacuum which was filled by the Clubmen. As a group they appeared first in Yorkshire, claiming to support neither side and concerned to protect property and people. Wessex, by 1645, was a stronghold of sympathy for them. Although their activities did not alter the course of things much, we see again that doggedness and straightforwardness of the rural person.

In 1685 James, Duke of Monmouth, landed in England, claiming that the English crown was rightfully his. At Taunton he was proclaimed king. His Monmouth Rebellion, sweeping through West Dorset, East Devon and Somerset, had an army that was never more than 8000 strong. These ill-armed farmers and cloth workers were challenged at Sedgemoor, where the 'Pitchfork' Rebellion was brought to an end by forces loyal to James II. The brutal Judge Jeffreys was sent as a travelling justice to administer quick and severe sentences on the captured followers of Monmouth. These became known as the 'Bloody Assizes'. Dame Alice Lisle, seventy years old at the time, was put to death because she had given a meal and a bed to two runaway men whom she did not even know. Jeffreys sentenced her to be burned alive. King James was 'merciful' and allowed her to be beheaded.

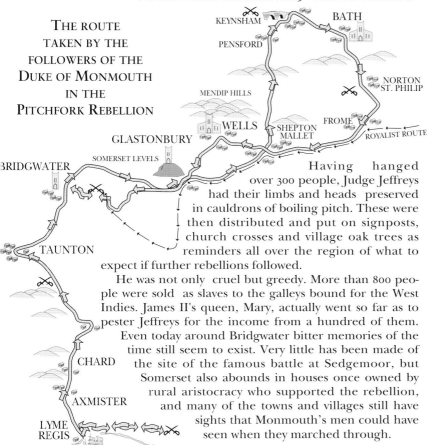

THE ROUTE
TAKEN BY THE
FOLLOWERS OF THE
DUKE OF MONMOUTH
IN THE
PITCHFORK REBELLION

Above:
*Judge Jefferies' house,
Dorchester.*

Having hanged over 300 people, Judge Jeffreys had their limbs and heads preserved in cauldrons of boiling pitch. These were then distributed and put on signposts, church crosses and village oak trees as reminders all over the region of what to expect if further rebellions followed.

He was not only cruel but greedy. More than 800 people were sold as slaves to the galleys bound for the West Indies. James II's queen, Mary, actually went so far as to pester Jeffreys for the income from a hundred of them. Even today around Bridgwater bitter memories of the time still seem to exist. Very little has been made of the site of the famous battle at Sedgemoor, but Somerset also abounds in houses once owned by rural aristocracy who supported the rebellion, and many of the towns and villages still have sights that Monmouth's men could have seen when they marched through.

William Gilpin in 1798 described THE GREAT BUSTARD *which inhabited Salisbury Plain. 'The only resident inhabitant of this vast waste is the bustard. This bird, which is the largest fowl we have in England, is fond of all extensive plains, and is found on several; but these are supposed to be his principal haunt. Here he breeds, and here he spends his summer-day, feeding with his mate on juicy berries, and the large dew-worms of the heath. As winter approaches, he forms into society. Fifty or sixty have been sometimes seen together.*

As the bustard leads his life in these unfrequented wilds, and studiously avoids the haunts of men, the appearance of any thing in motion, though at a considerable distance, alarms him. I know not that he is protected, like the partridge and pheasant, by any law: but his own vigilance is a better security to him than an act of parliament. As he is so noble a prize, his flesh so delicate, and the quantity of it so large, he is of course frequently the object of the fowler's stratagems. But his caution is generally a protection against them all. The scene he frequents, affords neither tree to shelter, nor hedge to screen, an enemy; and he is so tall, that when he raises his neck to take a perspective view, his eye circumscribes a very wide horizon. All open attempts therefore against him are fruitless'.

Eighteenth-Century Trade

COACH ROADS, CANALS AND MARKETS ENHANCED TRADE

Right:
Beau Nash,
Master of
Ceremonies at
Bath for 50
years, stands
in the Pump
Room.

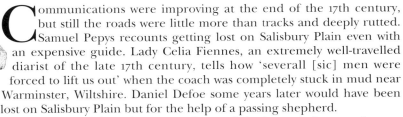

Communications were improving at the end of the 17th century, but still the roads were little more than tracks and deeply rutted. Samuel Pepys recounts getting lost on Salisbury Plain even with an expensive guide. Lady Celia Fiennes, an extremely well-travelled diarist of the late 17th century, tells how 'severall [sic] men were forced to lift us out' when the coach was completely stuck in mud near Warminster, Wiltshire. Daniel Defoe some years later would have been lost on Salisbury Plain but for the help of a passing shepherd.

By the end of the 18th century the roads had greatly improved, especially of course the great coach routes, such as London to Bristol and

Above:
George Cass, printer and bookbinder of Bridgwater, depicted by John Chubb in the late 18th century.

Above right:
An example of an 18th-century shop in Bridport.

Bath, London to Exeter, and London to Southampton. Also the canal network was coming into its own. The Kennet network allowed farm produce to go all the way from Newbury to London by barge. Commerce and trade benefited greatly and towns on the major routes grew accordingly. One indication of growth is the number of inns and coach houses that grew up along the routes and also the sizes of the markets and guildhalls. Good examples of all these can be found at Winchester, Bath, Salisbury, Malmesbury, Southampton, Yeovil and Exeter.

During the 18th century the range of crafts spread across Wessex is impressive and indicative of the continued importance of industry.

Carpet weaving at Wilton; glassmaking, brass foundries, at Bristol; coal mining in the Mendips; ironworks at Seend in Wiltshire and Gosport and Fontley in Hampshire; and a general spread of leatherworks, soapmakers, potteries, glovemakers, brick and pipe manufacturers, tobacco and snuff makers, paper mills, as well as the quarries that had been used since Saxon times at Chilmark (Wiltshire), Purbeck and Portland (Dorset), and Bath (Somerset). The quarries had tended to serve only local requirements. But, by the end of the 18th century transport and communications were improving quickly taking the stone further afield. This was all before the Mendips coal seams were worked out and the advent of the coal-based Industrial Revolution's shift to the richer and deeper seams of the North of England.

Crafts spread through Wessex

Above:
Thomas Whitty, of Axminster, Devon, began making hand-knotted carpets in 1755. In the following century, carpets of this type were made at the Wilton Carpet Factory, Wiltshire.

Bad Times on the Land

WAR, ENCLOSURES, BAD HARVESTS AND MECHANIZATION

Below:
'The Labourer's Plight,'
from G. Mitchell's The
Skeleton at the Plough,
*1874, highlights the low
wages and awful living
conditions of the rural
poor, such as the folk being
evicted (right) from their
cottage in Dorset in 1874.*

Farms were being consolidated in the 19th century, many smaller farms merging to make larger ones. Agricultural techniques were steadily improving and mechanization meant more work could be done by fewer men. Enclosure of land meant that the ordinary common land was again being swallowed up as had happened centuries before with the rule of the Normans. Common land provided grazing for peasant livestock, as well as foraging ground for fuel such as turf and wood. Without it these people had no means of subsistence.

The landowners prospered but the workers on the land did not. The French Wars and bad harvests at the start of the 19th century sent corn prices soaring beyond the reach of the common person. Bread, the staple food, was far too expensive. Hitherto even the poor had sneered at the potato as foreign food, but now it became part of their everyday diet.

Right:
*Animals were well fed and
treated better than farm
labourers.*

THE SWING RIOTS AND THE TOLPUDDLE MARTYRS, 1833

Would that staunch defender of the weak, William Cobbett, see a similarity now between what he observed in 1826 and the way in which one third of the world has more than enough and many of the rest barely subsist? 'I saw enough produce in five farm yards to feed twenty one parishes. But the infernal system causes it all to be carried away. Not a bit of good beef, or mutton, or veal and scarcely a bit of bacon is left for those who raise all this food and wool. For my own part I am really ashamed to ride a fat horse, to have a full belly, and to have a clean shirt upon my back while I look at these wretched countrymen of mine; while I actually see them reeling with weakness I am ashamed to reflect that they are my countrymen.' (*Rural Rides*, William Cobbett, near Warminster.) Four years later the Swing Riots broke out.

'Captain Swing' was an invented name used as a signature on letters to warn landowners and farmers of an impending attack. Threats of rickburning, destruction of farm machinery and revenge for the poverty and misery being suffered were the message. In the country areas far from major towns and law enforcement these would have been extremely frightening. Gangs of disaffected labourers went around at night to carry out their work.

The corn producing areas were the worst affected since if corn could not be worked there was nothing else. Again the land made the difference: 'Chalk was riotous, cheese was tranquil'. Thus Berkshire, Hampshire and Wiltshire were the worst hit, followed a little later by Dorset.

The riots were shortlived, at most a matter of months. The assizes imposed sentences ranging from fines and whipping to jail, death sentences, execution and transportation in an even shorter space of time.

At Dorchester the Tolpuddle Martyrs had their trial, in 1833, not for involvement in the Swing Riots but because of the magistrate's fearful memories of them. The men had set up a Friendly Society of Agricultural Labourers at Tolpuddle. James Frampton, the magistrate, sentenced them to transportation for this. A public outcry followed and they were brought back. Frampton had thus inadvertently made heroes of them.

Above:
Four of the six Tolpuddle Martyrs who survived transportation. Their ordeal is still remembered in Tolpuddle.

1883 the Tolpuddle Martyrs

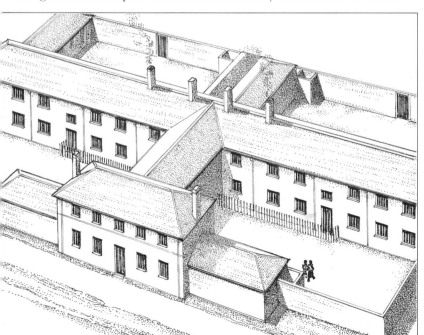

Left:
During the Swing Riots some Poor Houses, which represented the ultimate indignity, were attacked by those who had reason to fear them. This typical Poor House was at Andover.

The Coming of the Railways

The railways arrive

Above:

Box Tunnel near Bath was designed by that giant of the Industrial Revolution, Isambard Kingdom Brunel.

Less than a decade later unheard of changes were seen in Wessex. Mechanization was relentless. The railways had come. The 1840s saw routes from London go to Southampton, Bristol and Taunton. By 1850 Portsmouth, Gosport, Salisbury, Frome and Westbury were part of the network too. Exeter and many towns *en route* were opened up by 1860. The speed of commerce and trade was quicker than ever. The canals were badly hit being much slower than the railways. Agricultural produce, such as dairy products, became transported in raw bulk to the towns rather than treated and processed locally. So local small industries suffered. Wholesalers and middle men stepped into the commercial chain.

Again chalk was different from cheese. The railways helped the dairy farmer prosper. But they allowed the import and distribution of cheap grain from North America. The arable farmers suffered. Market gardeners benefited from the fast link to the huge London markets.

There were similar mixed effects on the manufacturing centres. If you were on a railway line you had a whole national market to aim at. If you were not – Cerne Abbas, Cranborne, Bere Regis – you began to fade away. With decline came a lack of local market fairs, which made the towns less interesting to the stage coach companies and so a downward

AND WEALTH TO SOME

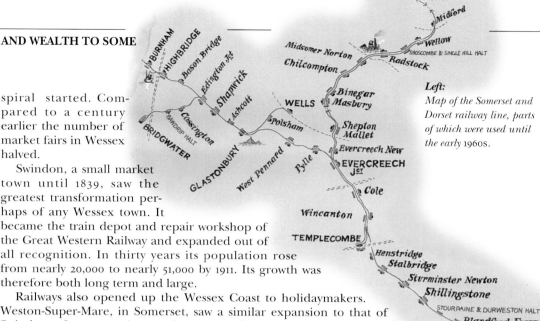

spiral started. Compared to a century earlier the number of market fairs in Wessex halved.

Swindon, a small market town until 1839, saw the greatest transformation perhaps of any Wessex town. It became the train depot and repair workshop of the Great Western Railway and expanded out of all recognition. In thirty years its population rose from nearly 20,000 to nearly 51,000 by 1911. Its growth was therefore both long term and large.

Railways also opened up the Wessex Coast to holidaymakers. Weston-Super-Mare, in Somerset, saw a similar expansion to that of Swindon. In 50 years its population went from 4,600 to nearly 19,500 by 1901. Southsea in Hampshire and Weymouth and Swanage in Dorset tell a similar story.

Left:
Map of the Somerset and Dorset railway line, parts of which were used until the early 1960s.

Left:
The Ocean Liner Express travelling from Southampton Docks to London, from a watercolour by Richard Wade (1956).

Below:
The railways brought excursion possibilities for all.

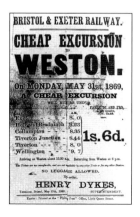

The War Office took advantage of the increased mobility given by the railways to open up Salisbury Plain for military training purposes. A branch line ran until recently from Grateley (still a commuter station on the main Exeter to London line) near Salisbury, through Newton Toney to Larkhill and Amesbury and even deeper into the Plain.

The major ports of Southampton and Portsmouth also had new injections of prosperity as a result of the steam engine. Bristol declined however. With the decline of its West Indies trade at the end of the 19th century already underway, it was unable to cope physically with the increased sizes of the new steamships. A new deep-water port has now been built at Avonmouth.

The cloth industry had gone into decline in Wessex from the end of the French Wars, probably because of the competition of cheaper goods from the north of England and from abroad. The railways came too late to offer any hope of new life.

Left:

A small country railway station in the early 1900s, which was axed with many others in the 1960s.

In the latter half of the 20th century the railways have changed again and electrification has made them an even faster means of transport than before. The industries of today are still very much tied to the land, the true resource of Wessex. Farming, though on ever larger consolidated farms, is all around. The huge growth industry of tourism is based on the land. Brewing is still important and, perhaps as a result of CAMRA (Campaign for Real Ale) activity, has had a new lease of life as many small breweries are opening up. Another area of growth is wine. This had largely died out in Britain since Roman times. Now the number of vineyards throughout Wessex is increasing every year.

The story of Wessex is one of change, resistance to change and then adapting to new ways whether brought by wild invading Saxon warriors 1500 years ago, or less bloodily by the steam engine. At the heart of Wessex is still the land itself. There will always be a big difference between chalk and cheese, and Wessex will always be a combination of the two.